Vegan Meal Prep
For Beginners

*50 Energy Boosting Vegan
Meals to control weight and
kickstart your heathy eating*

Jack Heffernan

TABLE OF CONTENTS

Introduction

There are many reasons to choose the vegan diet, also known as the plant-based lifestyle. You may choose it to improve your health, to lose weight, to reduce your environmental footprint or to increase the quality of your diet, or it may even be all of the above. Whatever your reasons for choosing the vegan lifestyle are, you will find that going vegan has many benefits to offer.

When most people hear about the vegan diet, they are worried about the protein component but eating vegan doesn't mean sacrificing protein (or flavor, for that matter).

There are a variety of foods and meals where vegans get their protein and energy. And no, you don't have to eat only tons of carrots sticks to achieve them.

When you remove animal-based proteins from your diet, it is important to replace them with healthy versions of plant-based proteins. There are many sources of these proteins that are also full of important vitamins, minerals, antioxidants, and phytonutrients.

Some great examples of vegan whole food vegan protein include:

- Lentils
- Beans and Chickpeas
- Tofu and Tempeh
- Seitan
- Quinoa
- Amaranth
- Chia Seeds
- Flaxseeds
- Sesame Seeds
- Sunflower and Pumpkin Seeds
- Nuts
- Oats, Wheat Berries, and Rice
- Spirulina

These 50 recipes are a mix of breakfasts, lunches, dinners, snacks and desserts that are suitable for those looking for some extra protein in their vegan diets, with healthy and gluten-free options too.

Lentil Bolognese

The lentils replicate meat in multiple ways in this dish. Not only do lentils provide protein and texture that is comparable to beef, but they also have a deep flavor that pairs well with the other ingredients in the sauce. You can enjoy this Bolognese over pasta, rice, spaghetti squash, or even zucchini noodles.

The Details:

The Number of Servings: 6

The Time Needed to Prepare: 10 minutes

The Time Required to Cook: 35 minutes

The Total Preparation/Cook Time: 45 minutes

Number of Calories in Individual Servings: 180

Protein Grams: 8

Fat Grams: 5

Total Carbohydrates Grams: 27

Net Carbohydrates Grams: 19

The Ingredients:

- Lentils, cooked – 2 cups
- Portobello mushroom – 1
- Sea salt – 1 teaspoon
- Onion, diced – 1
- Garlic, minced – 5 cloves
- Celery, chopped – 2 stalks
- Carrots, diced – 2
- Red bell pepper, diced – 1
- Olive oil – 2 tablespoons
- Crushed tomatoes – 2 cups
- Red wine, vegan variety - .75 cup
- Water - .75 cup
- Lemon juice – 1 tablespoon
- Brown sugar – 1 tablespoon
- Oregano, dried – 1 teaspoon

- Italian herb seasoning – 1 teaspoon
- Bay leaves – 2
- Black pepper, ground - .25 teaspoon
- Fresh parsley, chopped - .25 cup

The Instructions:

1. White, you can chop all of the vegetables by hand if you want to save time and energy you can also throw the white or yellow onion, Portobello mushrooms, black ground pepper, celery root stalks, carrots, and garlic cloves in a food processor together and set it on the pulse setting until they are finely diced.

2. On the stove set to a temperature of medium-high pour the olive oil into a large pot and add in the chopped vegetables and sea salt. While stirring occasionally, allow the vegetables to sauté for fifteen minutes. They will be slightly browned.

3. With your stove, lower the heating element to medium power and pour in the wine, stirring the contents occasionally until the wine has evaporated.

4. Add the crushed tomatoes, cooked lentils, water, and the remaining seasonings to the pot and stir until they have all combined. Reduce the heat to low and

allow the mixture to cook for twenty minutes, thickening slightly in the process.

5.   After cooking, remove the bay leaf from the pot. Using an immersion blender slightly pulse the ingredients so that it is only partially blended. You don't want the lentils to be fully pureed, only enough to thicken the Bolognese. If you do not have an immersion blender, you can use a regular stand blender.

6.   Serve the Bolognese immediately over pasta, or alternatively, you can also place it in the fridge to chill for up to a week. If you wait twenty-four hours before serving the Bolognese, you will find that the flavors of the sauce meld and deepen while stored in the fridge.

Crunchy Potato Tacos

Potatoes offer great flavor and texture to tacos, which pairs wonderfully with black beans for protein, fresh cilantro, diced tomatoes, and avocado. Enjoy these tacos as listed, or experiment with adding other favorite taco toppings.

The Details:

The Number of Servings: 4

The Time Needed to Prepare: 10 minutes

The Time Required to Cook: 25 minutes

The Total Preparation/Cook Time: 35 minutes

Number of Calories in Individual Servings: 654

Protein Grams: 21

Fat Grams: 19

Total Carbohydrates Grams: 103

Net Carbohydrates Grams: 85

The Ingredients:

- Potatoes, chopped – 1 pound
- Black beans, drained and rinsed – 15 ounces
- Bell pepper, diced – 1
- Romaine lettuce, chopped – 2 cups
- Avocado – 1
- Taco seasoning – 2 tablespoons
- Cilantro, fresh, chopped - .5 cup
- Roma tomato, diced - .5 cup
- Lime juice - .25 cup
- Flour tortillas, medium – 8
- Olive oil – 1 tablespoon

The Instructions:

1. Place the sliced and cubed potatoes in a pot that is large. Cover the cubed and sliced potatoes with water so that the water line is about one inch higher than the potatoes. Place this pot on the stove over high and allow it to reach a boil so that the bubbles are rolling and then reduce the heating element on

the stove to a medium. Allow the potatoes to cook at a high simmer in this way until fork-tender, about fifteen to twenty minutes. Drain off the water.

2.   In a skillet that is non-stick and large and on the stove over a heat of medium-high heat the olive oil. Once hot, add in the boiled potatoes, bell pepper, and taco seasoning. Stir this mixture together until the vegetables are well coated.

3.   After coating the vegetables in the seasonings, don't touch them for five to seven minutes so that they can sear. After about five minutes, lift the corner of one of the potatoes, and if it is crispy and golden, flip all the potatoes with a spatula and cook the second side for five to seven minutes until also crispy.

4.   While the potatoes cook, heat the black beans on the stove or in the microwave. Place the medium flour tortillas on a large dinner plate, cover the flour tortillas with a paper towel that has been damped with water, and microwave them for thirty seconds.

5.   To serve the tacos Fill each of the tortillas with the potatoes followed by the beans, lettuce, cilantro, avocado, and tomatoes. Top them off with a bit of the lime juice and then serve.

Meatless Loaf

Lentils are packed with protein and flavor, making them a great option for making a traditional vegan meatloaf. Try serving these with a side of mashed potatoes and green beans, and you will have a treat! It also tastes amazing when you use leftovers to make meatless loaf sandwiches.

The Details:

The Number of Servings: 6

The Time Needed to Prepare: 15 minutes

The Time Required to Cook: 50 minutes

The Total Preparation/Cook Time: 65 minutes

Number of Calories in Individual Servings: 227

Protein Grams: 11

Fat Grams: 3

Total Carbohydrates Grams: 40
Net Carbohydrates Grams: 31

The Ingredients:

- French lentils, cooked – 2 cups
- Button mushrooms, diced – 1.25 cup
- Onion, diced - .5
- Carrots, diced – 2
- Celery, diced – 2 stalks
- Ketchup - .33 cup
- Red bell pepper, diced - .5 cup
- Garlic, minced – 3 cloves
- Barbecue sauce – 1 tablespoon
- Brown sugar – 1 teaspoon
- Parsley, dried – 1 tablespoon
- Tomato paste – 2 tablespoons
- Sea salt - .5 teaspoon
- Quick oats - .5 cup
- Breadcrumbs, vegan - .5 cup
- Flaxseed meal – 2 tablespoons

The Instructions:

1. Preheat your oven to a temperature of Fahrenheit three-hundred and fifty degrees and then line a large aluminum baking sheet with kitchen parchment or a cooking mat made of silicone to prevent sticking.

2. Place the mushrooms, bell pepper, celery, carrots, and onion in a large stainless steel or non-stick skillet along with the sea salt and black ground pepper and allow them to sauté over medium heat until the root vegetables and mushrooms have become tender. Add in the minced garlic cloves and sauté for an extra minute before removing from the heat.

3. Place the cooked vegetables, lentils, tomato paste, oats, breadcrumbs, parsley, flaxseed meal, and barbecue sauce in the food processor. Slowly pulse the mixture until it forms a chunky dough. You want the vegetables to remain somewhat chunky, so don't puree it.

4. Form lentil mixture into a ball and then transfer it to the prepared baking sheet. Use your hands to reform the lentils into a loaf shape.

5.   Place the meatless loaf in the hot preheated oven and allow the loaf to roast for thirty-five minutes before removing it from the oven and top it with the sauce. To do this, spread the ketchup over the top and then sprinkle the brown sugar over it, as this will help it to caramelize. Return the meatless loaf with the sauce to the hot oven for ten minutes and then cool at room temperature of ten more minutes before slicing and serving.

Irish Stew

Whether it is winter, St. Patrick's Day, or simply a regular day of the week, you will love this traditional Irish stew. While this recipe calls for a can of stout beer, you can always leave the alcohol out and replace it with extra vegetable broth instead.

The Details:

The Number of Servings: 5

The Time Needed to Prepare: 10 minutes

The Time Required to Cook: 25 minutes

The Total Preparation/Cook Time: 35 minutes

Number of Calories in Individual Servings: 349

Protein Grams: 8

Fat Grams: 6

Total Carbohydrates Grams: 64

Net Carbohydrates Grams: 55

The Ingredients:

- Vegetable broth – 3 cups
- Onion, diced – 1
- Celery, diced – 2 stalks
- Garlic, minced – 5 cloves
- Carrots, sliced into bite-sized chunks – 3
- Parsnips, sliced into bite-sized chunks – 2
- Potatoes, sliced into bite-sized chunks – 2 large
- Brown sugar – 2 teaspoons
- Button mushrooms, quartered – 8 ounces
- Olive oil – 2 tablespoons
- Flour, all-purpose - .25 cup
- Stout beer, vegan – 1 can (optional, if not using replace with vegetable broth)
- Tomato paste - .5 cup
- Sea salt – 1.5 teaspoon
- Bay leaves – 2
- Thyme, dried – 1 teaspoon
- Black pepper, ground - .5 teaspoon

The Instructions:

1. Place a large stainless steel or ceramic pot on the stove and set it to medium-high heat. Into the large pot pour in the olive oil and allow it to heat up. Once it has preheated, add in the onion, celery, and garlic, letting it cook over the heat until they become tender and somewhat translucent, about five minutes.

2. Add the flour to the pot and stir it to coat the vegetables. Stir for about one minute until the flour begins to smell slightly nutty. Add in two cups of the vegetable broth and scrape at the bottom of the pan to remove any bits of food that have stuck.

3. Pour the beer, tomato paste, spices, and remaining vegetables into the pot. While the beer will bubble up at first, this is okay as they will disappear as the alcohol cooks off.

4. Bring the broth with the beer to bubble and simmer and allow it to do so for about fifteen minutes until the vegetables are fork tender. Don't let them overcook and become mushy.

5. The stew will be thick, as Irish stew traditionally is. But, if you like a thinner stew, feel free to add extra broth. Remove the bay leaves and serve.

Mushroom Stew with Mashed Potatoes

Mushrooms are known for having a deep flavor reminiscent of meat, all due to the natural chemical composition of the fungi that give them an umami flavor. The stew pairs perfectly with the accompanying creamy mashed potatoes, which taste buttery thanks to using Yukon Gold potatoes rather than russet.

The Details:

The Number of Servings: 6

The Time Needed to Prepare: 20 minutes

The Time Required to Cook: 2 hours

The Total Preparation/Cook Time: 140 minutes

Number of Calories in Individual Servings: 458

Protein Grams: 9

Fat Grams: 28

Total Carbohydrates Grams: 47

Net Carbohydrates Grams: 40

The Ingredients:

- Green beans – 1 cup
- Onion, diced – 1
- Carrots, diced – 2
- Garlic, minced – 1.5 tablespoons
- Button mushrooms, diced – 20 ounces
- Green peas – 1 cup
- Garlic powder - 1 teaspoon
- Potatoes, cubed – 1.5 cups
- Yukon Gold potatoes, cubed – 4 cups
- Flour, all-purpose – 5 tablespoons
- Olive oil – 5 tablespoons
- Parsley, fresh - .33 cup

- Tomato paste – 1.5 tablespoons
- Red wine, vegan – 1 cup
- Sea salt – 1.5 teaspoons
- Paprika - .5 teaspoon
- Thyme, dried – 1.5 teaspoon
- Black pepper, ground - .75 teaspoon
- Vegetable broth - .33 cup
- Vegan butter - .25 cup
- Sea salt – 1.25 teaspoon
- Chives, chopped – 2 tablespoons
- Vegetable broth – 4 cups

The Instructions:

1. Begin by placing a large pot on the stove and adding in two tablespoons of the olive oil, allowing it to preheat over medium heat. Once hot, add in the diced white onion and cook it over the heat until it becomes soft, about five to seven minutes. Add in the minced garlic cloves and cook for an additional minute.

2. While the onions cook, add the remaining three tablespoons of olive oil to a stainless-steel saucepan over a temperature of medium-low heat. Once the oil

has become warm, add in the all-purpose flour, and whisk until there are no lumps. Allow this mixture to cook for two to three minutes until it smells nutty. Slowly whisk in two cups of the vegetable broth until smooth.

3.   After the onions have softened add in the mushrooms, peas, green beans, carrots, potatoes, tomato paste, parsley, paprika, thyme, black pepper, and one and a half teaspoon of sea salt.

4.   Pour the red wine over the vegetable mixture and allow it to simmer for two minutes before adding in the flour/broth mixture and the remaining two cups of broth. Cover the pot and allow it to continue simmering on low for one and a half to two hours, occasionally giving it a good stir.

5.   Meanwhile, prepare the mashed potatoes. To do this, peel and cube the potatoes and then, once done, add them into a large stainless-steel pot of boiling water with added salt. Allow the potatoes to boil until fork-soft, about fifteen to twenty minutes.

6.   Drain off the water and transfer the potatoes to a large bowl and mash them with a potato masher. Stir in the one-third of a cup of broth, vegan butter, one

and a quarter teaspoon of sea salt, garlic powder, and chives. Adjust the seasonings to taste.

7.   To serve, divide the mashed potato between bowls for each serving and then top it off with the mushroom stew.

Sloppy Joes

Even kids will love these sloppy Joes, as they won't have any idea that they have lentils instead of meat. This filling freezes well, which means you can always store a batch in the freezer for last-minute meals.

The Details:

The Number of Servings: 4

The Time Needed to Prepare: 5 minutes

The Time Required to Cook: 10 minutes

The Total Preparation/Cook Time: 15 minutes

Number of Calories in Individual Servings: 351

Protein Grams: 17

Fat Grams: 6

Total Carbohydrates Grams: 58

Net Carbohydrates Grams: 46

The Ingredients:

- Onion – 1 tablespoon
- Lentils, cooked – 2.5 cups
- Garlic powder – 1 teaspoon
- Olive oil – 1 tablespoon
- Vegetable broth – 1 cup
- Balsamic vinegar – 1.5 teaspoon
- Black pepper, ground - .25 teaspoon
- Oregano, dried - .5 teaspoon
- Mustard powder – 1 teaspoon
- Sea salt - .5 teaspoon
- Cayenne pepper - .25 teaspoon
- Tomato paste – 4 tablespoons
- Burger buns, toasted – 4
- Chili powder -1 tablespoon

The Instructions:

1. Place a big stainless steel or non-stick kitchen pot on the stove set to a temperature of medium heat before adding in the olive oil and diced onion. Allow

the onion to sauté for about three minutes until it turns translucent.

2.   Add the cooked lentils, garlic powder, chili powder, sea salt, mustard powder, dried oregano, cayenne pepper, black pepper, and tomato paste to the pot. Stir it until it's fully combined and allow it to all cook together for three about three minutes.

3.   Stir the stock into the lentil mixture and allow it to simmer for a few minutes until it reaches your desired thickness. This will depend on personal preference.

4.   Remove the pot of lentil sloppy Joes from the heat of the stove, stir in the balsamic vinegar, and serve over the toasted buns.

Shepherd's Pie

This traditional Shepard's pie is made vegan thanks to the addition of mushrooms and walnuts. While Shepard's pie is always filled with vegetables, this one takes it to the next level to become a mouth-watering dish.

The Details:

The Number of Servings: 6

The Time Needed to Prepare: 20 minutes

The Time Required to Cook: 60 minutes

The Total Preparation/Cook Time: 80 minutes

Number of Calories in Individual Servings: 305

Protein Grams: 9

Fat Grams: 12

Total Carbohydrates Grams: 42

Net Carbohydrates Grams: 35

The Ingredients:

- Yukon gold potatoes, cut into chunks – 2 pounds
- Vegan butter – 1 tablespoon
- Green peas – 1 cup
- Dairy-free milk, unsweetened (soy, almond, or coconut) – .5 cup
- Sea salt – 1.5 teaspoon
- Onion, diced – 1
- Carrot, grated – 1
- Button mushrooms, finely diced – 1 pound
- Garlic, minced – 4 cloves
- Olive oil – 1.5 tablespoons
- Tomato paste – 1 tablespoon
- Vegetable broth – 1.25 cup
- Red wine, vegan - .5 cup
- Black pepper, ground - .25 teaspoon
- Rosemary, dried - .5 teaspoon

- Thyme, dried – 1 teaspoon
- Cornstarch – 1 tablespoon
- Walnuts, finely chopped – .75 cup
- Soy sauce – 2 tablespoons
- Sea salt – 1 teaspoon

The Instructions:

1. Place the Yukon gold potatoes cut into chunks into a large stainless-steel pot and cover them in water. Bring the water in the pot to a bubbling boil over a temperature of high heat and then lower the heat to medium-low to allow the potatoes to sit in a light simmer. Allow them to simmer until tender, about fifteen to twenty minutes.

2. Drain the simmering hot water off the Yukon gold potatoes and return them to the pot. Add in half of the dairy-free milk, vegan butter, ground black pepper, and one and a half teaspoons of sea salt. Mash the potatoes with a hand-held potato masher, slowly adding in the other half of the dairy-free milk as needed to reach the desired consistency. Be careful not to add too much liquid, as you don't want the potatoes to be too mushy or overly soft. Set aside.

3.   Preheat the oven to a temperature of Fahrenheit four-hundred degrees and prepare a nine-inch baking dish.

4.   Meanwhile, place a large stainless-steel skillet over a temperature of medium-high heat and add in the olive oil. Once hot, add in the mushrooms and sauté them until slightly browned and the liquid released from the vegetable has evaporated, about seven to eight minutes.

5.   Reduce the heat of the stove to medium and then add the grated carrots, diced onion, and minced garlic to the mushrooms and continue to sauté until the onions have softened, about four minutes. Stir in the tomato paste, soy sauce, and the herbs. Continue to cook this for a minute longer.

6.   Increase the heat of the skillet to medium-high and pour in the red wine. Allow it to nearly reduce completely, about three minutes.

7.   Once again, reduce the heat to medium. Dissolve the cornstarch into a small amount of the cold broth and then add in all the broth, the cornstarch mixture, and the walnuts to the skillet. Bring this mixture to a simmer and then let it continue simmering for about four minutes.

8.   Stir in the peas, sea salt, and pepper and allow it to simmer for two more minutes until the peas are hot.

9.   Spread the vegetable and broth mixture into the bottom of your dish and then top it with the mashed potatoes. Rake a fork over the top of the mashed potatoes to give them a little texture, which will allow it to toast better in the oven.

10. Bake the shepherd's pie in the preheated oven until hot all the way through, about twenty to thirty minutes. The last-minute, turn the oven to broiler to add a golden touch to the potatoes. Watch it carefully while under the broiler so that it doesn't burn.

Baked Ziti

You can use nearly any savory vegan sausage for this baked ziti, though the Italian sausage by Field Roast is especially good. In the same way, you can use any brand of vegan mozzarella shreds (or even homemade) that you prefer.

The Details:

The Number of Servings: 8

The Time Needed to Prepare: 15 minutes

The Time Required to Cook: 40 minutes

The Total Preparation/Cook Time: 55 minutes

Number of Calories in Individual Servings: 473

Protein Grams: 15

Fat Grams: 18

Total Carbohydrates Grams: 63

Net Carbohydrates Grams: 53

The Ingredients:

- Raw cashews – 1.5 cups
- Onion powder - .5 teaspoon
- Water - .75 cup
- Nutritional yeast - .25 cup
- Garlic, minced – 2 cloves
- Lemon juice – 2 tablespoons
- Sea salt – 1 teaspoon
- Ziti pasta – 1 pound
- Marinara sauce – 25 ounces
- Vegan sausage, sliced – 2
- Vegan Mozzarella shreds – 1.5 cups

The Instructions:

1. Preheat the oven to a temperature of Fahrenheit three-hundred and seventy-five degrees. Grease a nine-by-thirteen baking dish and set aside.
2. Prepare the pasta in the same way as written in the directions on the packaging it came in. Once

done, add the cooked pasta to the prepared baking dish.

3. Meanwhile, place the cashews in a saucepan, cover them with regular water, and bring it to a bubbling boil. Allow them to boil in the way for at least five minutes before draining off the water. Add the drained cashews to a blender along with the three-quarter cups of water, nutritional yeast, lemon juice, sea salt, onion powder, and minced garlic. Blend until the cashews become completely smooth, scraping the sides of the blender as needed. Set aside the sauce.

4. Pour the marinara sauce over the pasta and stir it together. Spread the pasta evenly across the pan. Spoon the cashew cheese sauce over the pasta and marinara, slightly stirring it together. Don't completely stir the pasta, as you want to leave pockets of cheese sauce between the noodles.

5. Sprinkle the vegan mozzarella shreds over the pasta and place it in the oven until hot and melted, about twenty-five minutes before serving.

Thai Green Curry

Green curry pairs perfectly with brown rice, which also adds a boost of protein and nutrition. However, you can also enjoy it with your favorite type of noodles. With a single serving of this curry, you can flood your body with nutrients and flavor, making it the perfect dish for when you might be coming down with a cold. Who needs chicken noodle soup when you can have this curry full of garlic, ginger, and peppers?

The Details:

The Number of Servings: 4

The Time Needed to Prepare: 5 minutes

The Time Required to Cook: 10 minutes

The Total Preparation/Cook Time: 15 minutes

Number of Calories in Individual Servings: 345

Protein Grams: 5

Fat Grams: 30

Total Carbohydrates Grams: 18

Net Carbohydrates Grams: 12

The Ingredients:

- Carrots, sliced – 2
- Red bell pepper, sliced – 1
- Olive oil – 2 tablespoons
- Green beans, cut into one-inch pieces – 10
- Broccoli florets – 1.5 cups
- Ginger, fresh, grated – 1 teaspoon
- Garlic, minced – 6 cloves
- Thai green chilies, minced – 1
- Green curry paste – 2 tablespoons
- Soy sauce – 2 teaspoons
- Coconut milk, full-fat – 13.5 ounces
- Brown sugar – 2 teaspoons
- Thai basil, fresh - .25 cup
- Sea salt - .5 teaspoon

The Instructions:

1. Begin by pouring half of the oil into a large pot and preheating it over medium-high heat. Once hot, add in the vegetables and allow them to cook in the oil for two minutes while stirring occasionally. Add in the minced garlic cloves and grated ginger root and cook for one more minute.

2. Into the vegetable, pot add in the green curry paste and sauté for two minutes while stirring. Stir in the coconut milk until it is fully combined. Allow it to continue to cook for six minutes until it is simmering, thick, and cream.

3. Stir in the soy sauce, brown sugar, sea salt, and Thai basil. Remove the pan from the heat. You can leave it thick or add a bit of water to loosen it if you want.

4. Serve the curry over rice. It will taste great immediately, but it will be even better after melding in the fridge for a day.

Cream of Broccoli Soup

This is a tasty soup that is easily prepared with plant-based ingredients. Broccoli is one of the top vegetables for cancer prevention, and a delicious flavor to add to many recipes. As a soup, this is an ideal treatment as a meal on its own, or as a side to a meal.

The Details:

The Number of Servings: 4

The Time Needed to Prepare: 5 minutes

The Time Required to Cook: 35 minutes

The Total Preparation/Cook Time: 40 minutes

The Ingredients:

1 medium broccoli floret, sliced and stem removed, cut into small pieces

2 cups of vegetable broth

1 cup of coconut milk

Sea salt

1 cup of potatoes, diced and peeled

Black pepper

The Instructions:

In a large cooking pot, add the vegetable broth, potatoes, and broccoli. Bring to a boil, then reduce heat and cook for another 10-15 minutes on medium, then add in the coconut milk, sea salt, and black pepper. Continue to cook and stir for another 20 minutes until all vegetables are thoroughly cooked and tender. Remove from heat and cool, then blend in the food processor in batches. Return the soup to the large cooking pot and reheat, then serve with rye bread and vegan butter.

If you want some options for this recipe, consider replacing the broccoli with cauliflower, or combine half of each in the soup. Carrots and yams can be added or substituted partially for the potatoes. Paprika, thyme, and sage are good options for this soup.

Avocado Pesto Pasta

While most pesto is made with olive oil, the pesto for this pasta uses everyone's favorite avocado. Avocado and olive oil have similar health benefits, as they contain the same types of fat, but the avocado has the added benefit of also containing vitamins and phytonutrients.

The Details:

The Number of Servings: 4

The Time Needed to Prepare: 5 minutes

The Time Required to Cook: 15 minutes

The Total Preparation/Cook Time: 20 minutes

Number of Calories in Individual Servings: 4o9

Protein Grams: 11

Fat Grams: 18

Total Carbohydrates Grams: 52

Net Carbohydrates Grams: 44

The Ingredients:

- Pasta – 8 ounces
- Spinach, frozen and thawed – 1 cup
- Avocado – 1
- Basil, fresh – 1.25 cups
- Olive oil – 2 tablespoons
- Garlic, minced – 4 cloves
- Sea salt - .5 teaspoon
- Lemon juice – 2 tablespoons
- Cashews, raw - .25 cup
- Black pepper, ground - .25 teaspoon

The Instructions:

1. Prepare the pasta in the same way as written in the directions on the packaging it came in before draining off the water.

2. Meanwhile, place all the other ingredients called for above in the blender or food processor and blend on high until it becomes smooth and can spread easily.

3.   Taste the pesto and adjust salt to taste. Once it fits your preference, toss the pasta with the pesto, and serves alone or with a side of sliced cherry tomatoes.

Spring Rolls

Spring rolls are easy to make, especially with this recipe that only requires a few ingredients on hand! You can experiment with enjoying these with a variety of dipping sauces, but I recommend Thai sweet chili sauce.

The Details:

The Number of Servings: 5

The Time Needed to Prepare: 10 minutes

The Time Required to Cook: 5 minutes

The Total Preparation/Cook Time: 15 minutes

Number of Calories in Individual Servings: 286

Protein Grams: 4

Fat Grams: 7

Total Carbohydrates Grams: 49

Net Carbohydrates Grams: 44

The Ingredients:

- Rice paper wrappers – 10
- Rice noodles – 200 grams
- Broccoli sprouts - .5 cup
- Avocado, thinly sliced – 1
- Zucchini, spiralized – 1
- Carrots, spiralized – 3
- Bell pepper, thinly sliced – 1
- Sesame seeds, toasted – 2 tablespoons

The Instructions:

1. Prepare the rice noodles in the same way as written in the directions on the packaging it came in. Once done, drain, rinse the noodles under cold water, and drain again. Meanwhile, prepare the vegetables.

2. Meanwhile, pour some hot water in a large bowl and put the rice papers in the bowl so that they are completely covered by water. Allow the paper to soak for fifteen seconds until soft.

3. Cover a cutting board with a wet paper towel to prevent sticking, and then on top of the wet paper

towel, place one of the wet rice wrappers. In the center of the wrapper place, one-tenth of the prepared vegetables and cooked noodles. Don't get the filling too close to the edges to leave room to roll it up.

4.   Roll up the spring rolls the same way as you would a burrito. To do this, first, fold the ends over the edge of the vegetables and then roll them up, starting at one side until it is a neat and tightly rolled bundle. Place the roll on a plate and continue to fill and roll the remaining nine.

5.   Serve the spring rolls with soy sauce, Thai sweet chili sauce, peanut sauce, or any of your other favorite dipping sauces.

Potato Roasted Brussels Sprouts

These potatoes and Brussels sprouts offer not only a healthy side dish to nearly any meal, but they will also keep you satisfied for hours to come. With both minced garlic and garlic powder, you will love the punch of flavor!

The Details:

The Number of Servings: 5

The Time Needed to Prepare: 7 minutes

The Time Required to Cook: 40 minutes

The Total Preparation/Cook Time: 47 minutes

Number of Calories in Individual Servings: 270

Protein Grams: 5

Fat Grams: 11

Total Carbohydrates Grams: 39

Net Carbohydrates Grams: 33

The Ingredients:

- Baked potatoes, peeled – 2 pounds
- Brussels sprouts, sliced in half – 2 cups
- Garlic, minced – 5 cloves
- Garlic powder – 3 teaspoons
- Onion, diced – 1 cup
- Sea salt – 1 teaspoon
- Black pepper, ground - .25 teaspoon
- Olive oil - .25 cup

The Instructions:

1. Preheat the oven to a temperature of Fahrenheit four-hundred and twenty-five degrees and prepare a large baking sheet.

2. Place the whole peeled russet potatoes in a pot that is large and full of water. Bring the water to a boil and allow them to simmer for fifteen to twenty minutes. Don't cook the potatoes until fork tender. You only want them partially cooked.

3. Drain off the water and allow the potatoes to cool until you can easily handle them. Slice the partially baked potatoes into inch-size chunks.

4. On a large baking sheet, heat half of the olive oil along with the Brussels sprouts, onion, and garlic. Allow the vegetables to sauté over a temperature of medium-low heat for a period of ten minutes, until lightly golden and browned.

5. Toss together the remaining oil with the potatoes and garlic powder and add them to the pan along with the Brussels sprouts. Cook for an additional fifteen minutes, until the potatoes have crisped up.

Chickpea Salad Pinwheels

These pinwheels are the perfect lunch to enjoy on-the-go, as you can easily assemble them the night before or morning of, pack them in a lunchbox, and enjoy them at work or even on a picnic.

The Details:

The Number of Servings: 4

The Time Needed to Prepare: 10 minutes

The Time Required to Cook: 0 minutes

The Total Preparation/Cook Time: 10 minutes

Number of Calories in Individual Servings: 390

Protein Grams: 13

Fat Grams: 17

Total Carbohydrates Grams: 48

Net Carbohydrates Grams: 35

The Ingredients:

- Chickpeas drained and rinsed – 30 ounces
- Red onion, diced - .5
- Jalapeno, minced – 1
- Avocado – 1
- Vegan mayonnaise - .25 cup
- Dijon mustard - .25 cup
- Sea salt - .5 teaspoon
- Baby spinach – 1 cup
- Tortillas, large – 2
- Sea salt - .5 teaspoon

The Instructions:

1. Into a kitchen, bowl, add the chickpeas and mash them with a fork. Add in the avocado and continue to mash with the fork until creamy and combined.

2. Stir the hot sauce, Dijon mustard, vegan mayonnaise, black pepper, red onion, jalapeno, and sea salt into the bowl and stir to combine, tasting and adjusting the seasoning to your preference.

3. Place the chickpea salad in the fridge and allow it to chill for at least thirty minutes, or up to a day.

4.   To assemble, lay out both tortillas and divide the chickpea filling between the two of them. Spread of the filling to the edges of the tortillas. Sprinkle the spinach over one side of each tortilla.

5.   Staring at the side with the spinach, grab the tortillas and roll them up tightly until they are fully rolled. Use a knife and cut each tortilla into eight pieces to form sliced pinwheels. Serve the chickpea salad pinwheels immediately or store them in the fridge to chill until ready to eat.

6.   Alternatively, you could slice eat tortilla in half after rolling them up and serve it like a burrito.

Sweet and Sour Chickpeas

When you want to enjoy old favorite dishes, that typically involve meat, you don't have to buy meat replacements. The truth is that many inexpensive ingredients you already find in your pantry, such as chickpeas, are a great option to replace meats. Not only are they healthy, they are also filling and full of protein.

The Details:

The Number of Servings: 3

The Time Needed to Prepare: 3 minutes

The Time Required to Cook: 10 minutes

The Total Preparation/Cook Time: 13 minutes

Number of Calories in Individual Servings: 311

Protein Grams: 14

Fat Grams: 4

Total Carbohydrates Grams: 54

Net Carbohydrates Grams: 42

The Ingredients:

- Chickpeas drained and rinsed – 30 ounces
- Soy sauce - .25 cup
- Garlic, minced – 2 cloves
- Green beans, trimmed – 7 ounces
- Cornstarch – 1 tablespoon
- Brown sugar – 2 tablespoons
- Rice vinegar – .25 cup
- Water - .5 cup
- Tomato paste – 1 tablespoon

The Instructions:

1. Add the garlic into a non-stick skillet and allow it to sauté over medium heat for two minutes or until fragrant and golden. Add in the green beans and continue to sauté for three minutes, until softened.

2. Meanwhile, whisk together the brown sugar, soy sauce, rice vinegar, water, cornstarch, and tomato paste in a separate container.

3.   Pour the sauce mixture and chickpeas to the hot skillet and continue to cook on medium-low heat until the sauce has thickened about five minutes. Serve alone or overcooked rice.

Thai Quinoa Bowls

These quinoa bowls offer a punch of flavor and nutrition with all your favorite Thai ingredients complementing each other. While salads are often difficult to prepare ahead of time due to it being easy for lettuce to become wilted, with these bowls having a base of quinoa and sturdy vegetables, you won't have to worry about wilting. Make these bowls immediately before serving, or up to three days in advance.

The Details:

The Number of Servings: 1

The Time Needed to Prepare: 5 minutes

The Time Required to Cook: 0 minutes

The Total Preparation/Cook Time: 5 minutes

Number of Calories in Individual Servings: 372

Protein Grams: 15

Fat Grams: 17

Total Carbohydrates Grams: 43

Net Carbohydrates Grams: 34

The Ingredients:

- Quinoa, cooked - .5 cup
- Sesame seed oil – 1 tablespoon
- Red onion, diced - .5 cup
- Lime juice – 2 tablespoons
- Broccoli, finely diced - .5 cup
- Carrots, grated - .25 cup
- Green onions, chopped - .25 cup
- Cilantro, fresh, chopped - .25 cup
- Peanuts, chopped – 2 tablespoons
- Soy sauce – 1 tablespoon
- Lime zest – .5 teaspoon

- Sesame seeds – 1 teaspoon
- Rice vinegar – 1 tablespoon
- Garlic, minced – 2 cloves
- Garlic, grated - .25 teaspoon

The Instructions:

1. In a large kitchen bowl, toss together the diced red onion, chopped green onions, grated carrots, diced broccoli, chopped cilantro, cooked quinoa, and peanuts.

2. In a small bowl, whisk together the sesame seed oil, soy sauce, lime juice and zest, sesame seeds, rice vinegar, garlic, and ginger. Pour this mixture over the salad and toss it together before serving.

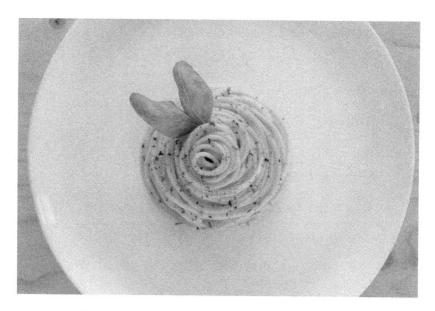

Pumpkin and Sage Pasta

You will feel like you are at a gourmet restaurant with this pumpkin and rubbed sage pasta that is complemented with garlic, cinnamon, and a hint of cayenne. Of course, you can omit the cayenne if you are extra sensitive to the pepper.

The Details:

The Number of Servings: 4

The Time Needed to Prepare: 5 minutes

The Time Required to Cook: 25 minutes

The Total Preparation/Cook Time: 30 minutes

Number of Calories in Individual Servings: 489

Protein Grams: 4

Fat Grams: 24

Total Carbohydrates Grams: 61

Net Carbohydrates Grams: 52

The Ingredients:

- Pasta – 8 ounces
- Coconut milk, full-fat – 14 ounces
- Pumpkin puree – 16 ounces
- Vegetable broth – 3 tablespoons
- Red onion, diced – 1
- Garlic, minced – 3 cloves
- White wine - .5 cup
- Black pepper, ground - .125 teaspoon
- Cayenne pepper - pinch
- Cinnamon - .25 teaspoon
- Sage, fresh, rubbed and chopped – 1 tablespoon
- Nutritional yeast – 1 tablespoon
- Nutmeg - .125 teaspoon
- Sea salt - .5 teaspoon

The Instructions:

1. Prepare the pasta according to the manufacturer's instructions. Once done, drain off the water.

2. In a large saucepan, add in the vegetable broth and red onion, allowing it to sauté over a hot temperature on the stove of medium heat until the onion is semi-transparent, about five minutes. Add in the white wine and deglaze the pan, allowing it to simmer until most of the liquid is cooked off, about three minutes.

3. Into the skillet, add the garlic, fresh sage, nutritional yeast, sea salt, cinnamon, nutmeg, black pepper, and cayenne pepper. Allow this to all cook together for about two minutes to allow the flavors to meld.

4. Stir the pumpkin puree and coconut milk into the skillet until the ingredients are fully combined. Reduce the heat of the stove to that of a medium-low and allow the pumpkin sauce to simmer for about five minutes.

5. Toss the pasta with the pumpkin sauce and serve immediately.

Wild Rice Soup

Wild rice has a lot more health benefits than other kinds of rice, due to its large supply of vitamins and minerals. But, not only does it have superior nutrition, but it also increased flavor. You will love the nutty flavor it imparts on this soup.

The Details:

The Number of Servings: 4

The Time Needed to Prepare: 10 minutes

The Time Required to Cook: 60 minutes

The Total Preparation/Cook Time: 70 minutes

Number of Calories in Individual Servings: 364

Protein Grams: 10

Fat Grams: 11

Total Carbohydrates Grams: 59

Net Carbohydrates Grams: 45

The Ingredients:

- Vegetable broth – 6 cups
- Onion, diced – 1
- Celery, diced – 2 stalks
- Carrots, diced – 2
- Button mushrooms, sliced – 8 ounces
- Sweet potato, diced – 1
- Garlic, minced – 5 cloves
- Wild rice, uncooked – 1 cup
- Dairy-free milk, unsweetened (soy, almond, or coconut) – 1.5 cup
- Olive oil – 3 tablespoons
- Flour, all-purpose - .25 cup
- Sea salt – 1.5 teaspoon
- Bay leaf – 1
- Sage, dried - .5 teaspoon
- Thyme, dried - .5 teaspoon
- Black pepper, ground - .25 teaspoon
- Kale, chopped – 1.5 cups

The Instructions:

1.   Pour in the one tablespoon of olive oil to a large stainless-steel cooking pot on the stove and sauté the onion over medium-high heat for about five minutes, until see-through and tender. Add in the garlic and cook for two additional minutes until fragrant.

2.   Into the pot stir the sweet potato, carrots, celery, mushrooms, wild rice, vegetable stock, bay leaf, sea salt, sage, thyme, and black pepper. Allow the broth to reach a simmer before reducing the heat to a temperature of medium-low. Continue to let the liquid bubble lightly for a period of forty-five minutes while stirring with a spoon occasionally.

3.   Meanwhile, after the soup has been cooking for thirty-five minutes, prepare the cream cause. To do this, put the remaining two tablespoons of olive oil and flour in a saucepan. Cook for about one minute before gradually whisking in the dairy-free milk. Continue to cook until it has thickened and reaches a simmer.

4.   Whisk the cream sauce and kale into the soup and continue to cook the soup for about five more minutes, until the kale is wilted. Enjoy while hot.

Tofu Buffalo Wings

Just because you are vegan doesn't mean you can't enjoy your favorite foods, only that you need to find new ways to enjoy the same flavors and textures. This recipe uses tofu instead of chicken wings, which is a great carrier for the hot sauce. Try serving this with a dairy-free Ranch, and you will be in love.

The Details:

The Number of Servings: 4

The Time Needed to Prepare: 20 minutes

The Time Required to Cook: 30 minutes

The Total Preparation/Cook Time: 50 minutes

Number of Calories in Individual Servings: 351

Protein Grams: 16

Fat Grams: 19

Total Carbohydrates Grams: 30

Net Carbohydrates Grams: 28

The Ingredients:

- Tofu, extra firm – 1 pound
- Cornstarch – 6 tablespoons
- Soy milk - .25 cup
- Panko bread crumbs, dairy-free – 1 cup
- Sea salt - .5 teaspoon
- Parsley, fresh, minced – 1 tablespoon
- Olive oil – 2 tablespoons
- Black pepper, ground - .25 teaspoon
- Vegan Butter (Earth Balance) – 3 tablespoons
- Franks Hot Sauce – 6 tablespoons
- Garlic powder - .125 teaspoon
- Sea salt – .125 teaspoon

The Instructions:

1.   Preheat your oven to a temperature of Fahrenheit four-hundred and twenty-five degrees and then grease a large baking sheet with olive oil before setting it aside.

2.   Before using the tofu, prepare it by pressing out the excess water. You can do this best by using a tofu press, but if you do not have one on hand, you can place it between a couple of dinner plates with some paper towels to absorb the liquid and then place a heavy-weight pot or cast-iron skillet on top of the plates. Allow the tofu to press for twenty to thirty minutes before using it.

3.   Once the tofu has been pressed, cut it into half-inch sticks or into eighteen pieces of approximately equal size. To do this, you can slice the block into six slices widthwise and then lengthwise slice it three times.

4.   Grab three small bowls and into each one put individually the Cornstarch, breadcrumbs, and dairy-free milk. Into the bowl with the breadcrumbs also mix in the half teaspoon of sea salt, black pepper, and parsley. Add a small portion of this bread crumb mixture onto a dinner plate or saucer.

5.   Dip each slice of tofu first into the cornstarch, then the dairy-free milk, and lastly, place it on the plate with breadcrumbs and ensure it becomes fully and evenly coated. Once you are done coating the tofu, place the coated slice on the prepared baking sheet and continue to coat the remaining slices.

6.   Place the aluminum baking sheet with the coated tofu in the prepared oven and bake the tofu slices first for twenty-five minutes before using a spatula to gently flip them over and then bake for an additional fifteen minutes until they become crispy.

7.   While the tofu bakes melt the vegan butter and combine it with the hot sauce, garlic powder, and remaining sea salt.

8.   Serve the buffalo tofu immediately with the butter dipping sauce or save them for later and reheat in the oven so that they become crispy again.

Mongolian "Beef"

This faux beef is made with seitan, which is a meat replacement made with wheat gluten. You will be surprised how similar the texture and flavor of seitan is to meat when you prepare it correctly! It makes a wonderful alternative to all your old favorite dishes.

The Details:

The Number of Servings: 8

The Time Needed to Prepare: 3 minutes

The Time Required to Cook: 17 minutes

The Total Preparation/Cook Time: 20 minutes

Number of Calories in Individual Servings: 318

Protein Grams: 44

Fat Grams: 5

Total Carbohydrates Grams: 24

Net Carbohydrates Grams: 24

The Ingredients:

- Olive oil – 1.5 tablespoons
- Olive oil – 2 teaspoons
- Seitan, sliced into 1-inch pieces – 1 pound
- Soy sauce, low sodium - .5 cup
- Water, cold – 2 tablespoons
- Cornstarch – 2 teaspoons
- Garlic, minced – 3 cloves
- Ginger, grated - .5 teaspoon
- Red pepper flakes - .5 teaspoon
- Brown sugar - .5 cup
- Chinese five-spice - .25 teaspoon
- Green onions, sliced – 2 stalks
- Sesame seeds, toasted – 1 tablespoon

The Instructions:

1. Begin by preparing the sauce in a small stainless-steel saucepan on the stove set to a temperature of medium heat. To do this, add the ginger and garlic to the pan and stir it constantly for thirty seconds to prevent burning. After thirty seconds are up, add in the Chinese five-spice powder and red pepper flakes before cooking for an additional thirty to sixty seconds while stirring. It is ready when the spices become fragrant.

2. Into the saucepan, add the soy sauce and brown sugar and stir to dissolve the sugar. Reduce the heat of the saucepan to a heat of medium-low and allow it to bubble and simmer until the sauce as slightly reduced, about five to seven minutes.

3. In a small glass or metal kitchen bowl or cup, whisk together the cornstarch with the cold water until it is dissolved without any clumps. Quickly whisk this slurry into the Mongolian sauce and continue to cook the mixture for a full two to three minutes. The sauce is ready when it has thickened slightly and become glossy. Reduce the heat of the stove to warm to keep the sauce warm without cooking it further.

4. In a large skillet over a temperature of medium-high, add the olive oil and allow it to heat until it

shimmers but before it smokes. Add in the sliced seitan and allow it to cook until it becomes crispy around the edges and slightly browned about four to five minutes.

5.   Reduce the heat of the skillet to low and then pour in the prepared Mongolian sauce and the sliced green onions. Toss the seitan in the sauce and cook it for a few minutes so that all the seitan is evenly coated, and the sauce sticks to it.

6.   Remove the seitan and from the stove, sprinkle the sesame seeds over the top, and serve immediately with rice or vegetables.

Lentil Curry

This lentil curry is a complete source of protein as it is prepared with heart-healthy lentils and brown rice. While this dish is flavorful on its own from the mixture of fragrant spices, it is even better when you serve it with a bit of fresh basil and a wedge of lime.

The Details:

The Number of Servings: 5

The Time Needed to Prepare: 5 minutes

The Time Required to Cook: 50 minutes

The Total Preparation/Cook Time: 55 minutes

Number of Calories in Individual Servings: 531

Protein Grams: 18

Fat Grams: 22

Total Carbohydrates Grams: 70

Net Carbohydrates Grams: 58

The Ingredients:

- Vegetable broth – 3 cups
- Chopped tomatoes, canned – 28 ounces
- Turmeric - .5 teaspoon
- Coconut milk, full-fat – 14 ounces
- Garlic, minced – 1 teaspoon
- Brown lentils, dried – 1.5 cups
- Coriander, ground - .5 teaspoon
- Basil, fresh – 2 cups
- Onion, diced – 1
- Brown sugar – 1 tablespoon
- Sea salt – 2 teaspoons
- Curry powder, mild – 1 tablespoon
- Olive oil – 2 tablespoons
- Cumin - .5 teaspoon
- Black pepper, ground - .25 teaspoon
- Brown rice, cooked – 3 cups
- Cayenne pepper - .25 teaspoon

The Instructions:

1. Into a large heavy-bottom and stainless steel or ceramic pot add the olive oil along with the diced onion, curry powder, cumin, cayenne pepper, turmeric, coriander, and garlic. Allow this mixture to cook over medium until the onion has softened, and the spices have become fragrant.

2. Add the lentils, canned tomatoes, coconut milk, and vegetable broth to the pot and stir until the mixture is well combined. Increase the heat to high heat to bring the liquid to a boil.

3. Once the broth has begun to boil lower the heat of the stove to a low temperature, cover the pot with a tight-fitting lid, and allow it to simmer for thirty to forty minutes until the lentils have become soft. Be sure to stir the curry occasionally during the cooking process.

4. After the lentils have softened stir in the fresh basil, brown sugar, sea salt, and black pepper. Give the basil a minute or two to wilt before serving.

5. When serving, divide the cooked rice between the bowls, top with the lentil curry, and garnish with a bit of basil and lime.

BBQ Tempeh Ribs

These ribs are made with tempeh, which is not only full of protein but also provides you with an amazing texture and slightly nutty flavor, perfect to compliment the barbecue rub and of your favorite sauces.

The Details:

The Number of Servings: 3

The Time Needed to Prepare: 5 minutes

The Time Required to Cook: 35 minutes

The Total Preparation/Cook Time: 40 minutes

Number of Calories in Individual Servings: 252

Protein Grams: 22

Fat Grams: 12

Total Carbohydrates Grams: 18

Net Carbohydrates Grams: 17

The Ingredients:

- Tempeh – 12 ounces
- Black pepper, ground - .75 teaspoon
- Onion powder - .5 teaspoon
- Apple juice – 2 tablespoons
- Paprika, smoked – 1 tablespoon
- Brown sugar – 2 teaspoons
- Garlic powder - .5 teaspoon
- Chili powder – 2 teaspoons
- Cayenne pepper - .125 teaspoon
- Sea salt – 2 teaspoons

The Instructions:

1. Slice the tempeh into rib-like strips, approximately six inches long and one inch wide each. Brush the strips with the apple juice so that they are fully coated in all the pores between the beans. This will allow the rub to fully adhere to the tempeh.

2. Combine all the seasonings and brown sugar together into a rub mixture and then coat the tempeh slices with this rub, being sure that the entire surface of each strip is coated.

3. Either roast the ribs in the oven set to three-hundred and fifty-degrees for thirty-five minutes or grill them. To grill, the ribs, place them on indirect heat away from the coals at a low heat and use hickory chips for added flavor. During the grilling process, occupationally brush the ribs with apple juice to prevent drying.

4. Five minutes before the ribs are done, roasting or grilling coat them in your favorite barbecue sauce and allow them to cook for a few more minutes to form a nice crust.

Decadent Chili

Great chili doesn't need meat. You will find that this chili packs the same flavor and texture you want, but with beans instead of beef. When topped with savory tofu crumbles, it is to die for.

The Details:

The Number of Servings: 6

The Time Needed to Prepare: 5 minutes

The Time Required to Cook: 30 minutes

The Total Preparation/Cook Time: 35 minutes

Number of Calories in Individual Servings: 417

Protein Grams: 27

Fat Grams: 8

Total Carbohydrates Grams: 67

Net Carbohydrates Grams: 47

The Ingredients:

- Kidney beans, drained and rinsed – 15 ounces
- Nutritional yeast – 2 tablespoons
- Chili powder – 3 tablespoons
- Crushed tomatoes – 56 ounces
- Water – 1 cup
- Onion, diced – 1
- Soy sauce – 2 tablespoons
- Garlic, minced – 5 cloves
- Cayenne pepper - .25 teaspoon
- Brown sugar – 1 tablespoon
- Cocoa powder – 1 tablespoon
- Black beans, drained and rinsed – 30 ounces
- Paprika, smoked – 1 teaspoon
- Sea salt – 1 teaspoon
- Tofu, extra firm – 14 ounces
- Paprika, smoked – 1 teaspoon

The Instructions:

1.   First, start by making the tofu crumbles to serve with the chili. To do this line, a large aluminum baking sheet with kitchen parchment or a cooking silicone mat and preheat your oven to a temperature of Fahrenheit three-hundred and fifty degrees.

2.   In a large bowl, mix a paste of nutritional yeast, one teaspoon of smoked paprika, chili powder, and the soy sauce. Use your hands and crumble the firm tofu into the bowl along with the pate, and then use a spoon to combine together the mixture together until the tofu is fully coated in the paste.

3.   Spread the seasoned tofu evenly over the readied aluminum baking sheet and allow it to roast in the oven for thirty minutes. Halfway through the cooking process, stir the tofu mixture to allow for even cooking.

4.   Meanwhile, begin the chili by placing a large pot on the stove set to medium heat. Add in a couple of tablespoons of water and the diced onion and sauté for about five minutes until the onion has become transparent. Add in the garlic and continue to sauté for one more minute while you stir, until the garlic is

fragrant. If the water evaporates, add a bit more so that you can prevent burning.

5.   Add all the remaining ingredients for the chili, aside from the tofu crumbles, to the pot and stir it until fully combined. Increase the heat so that the ingredients reach a boil over a temperature of high heat, and once the chili begins to bubble, lower the stove heat to a low bubbling simmer. Allow this mixture to simmer for twenty minutes while the tofu crumbles bake in the oven.

6.   After the tofu crumbles are removed from the oven, add them into the pot with the chili and serve the chili plain or with your favorite vegan chili toppings. Some great options include vegan cheese shreds, dairy-free sour cream, diced tomatoes, cilantro, and corn chips.

Tofu Omelet

Just because you don't eat eggs doesn't mean you can't enjoy a good omelet! This recipe uses a mixture of vegetables for the filling, but feel free to customize it with all your favorite omelet fillings.

The Details:

The Number of Servings: 1

The Time Needed to Prepare: 10 minutes

The Time Required to Cook: 20 minutes

The Total Preparation/Cook Time: 30 minutes

Number of Calories in Individual Servings: 361

Protein Grams: 15

Fat Grams: 26

Total Carbohydrates Grams: 20

Net Carbohydrates Grams: 16

The Ingredients:

- Tofu, silken, patted dry – 5 ounces
- Hummus – 2 tablespoons
- Water – 1 tablespoon
- Olive oil – 4 teaspoons, divided
- Sea salt - .5 teaspoon
- Nutritional yeast – 2 tablespoons
- Garlic, minced – 2 cloves
- Cornstarch – 1 teaspoon
- Paprika - .25 teaspoon
- Black pepper, ground - .125 teaspoon
- Onion, minced – 2 tablespoons
- Kale, chopped - .25 cup
- Mushrooms, sliced - .25 cup
- Tomato, diced – 3 tablespoons

The Instructions:

1.   Preheat your oven to a temperature of three-hundred and seventy-five-degrees Fahrenheit.

2.   Over medium heat place a medium-sized and oven-safe skillet on the stove. After it has preheated,

add in two teaspoons of your olive oil and minced garlic, allowing it to sauté for a minute while stirring until it becomes fragrant and golden in color.

3.   Place the sautéed garlic, tofu, water, hummus, nutritional yeast, paprika, black pepper, and cornstarch into a food processor or blender. Blend this mixture until smooth, scraping down the size occasionally, as needed.

4.   Into the skillet on the stove, add the minced onion, kale, and mushrooms. Sauté these over medium heat for about five minutes, until the onion is transparent. If needed, add a bit of water to prevent burning. Remove the vegetables from the skillet and set aside.

5.   Add the remaining two teaspoons of olive oil to the skillet and allow it to fully coat the bottom. Back to the skillet, add one-quarter of the cooked vegetables before pouring the tofu omelet batter over the top. Use a silicone spatula to carefully spread the tofu batter over the entire pan, being careful to not cause gaps or holes in it.

6.   Continue to cook the tofu omelet for five minutes, until the edges begin to look dry. Place the skillet in the preheated oven and allow it to bake until golden-

brown, about ten to fifteen minutes. Keep in mind that the longer it cooks, the drier and well done it will be. Therefore, the cooking time varies based on personal preference.

7.   During the last few minutes of baking time in the oven, add the remaining roasted vegetables on top and allow it to finish cooking until they are warmed through.

8.   Remove the omelet from the stove and gently fold the omelet over with a spatula so that the vegetables are fully encased by the tofu "egg". If you have trouble flipping the omelet simply serve the dish as a scramble or frittata.

9.   Top the omelet off with the freshly diced tomato and enjoy.

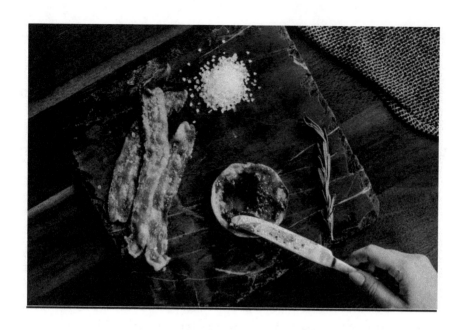

Tempeh Bacon

One food that many people are hesitant to give up when going vegan is bacon. But just because you choose to not eat meat doesn't mean you can't enjoy your favorite flavors and textures. This tempeh bacon offers the salty-sweet flavor we all know and love, while also having the same crispiness of bacon.

The Details:

The Number of Servings: 4

The Time Needed to Prepare: 5 minutes

The Time Required to Cook: 15 minutes

The Total Preparation/Cook Time: 20 minutes

Number of Calories in Individual Servings: 270

Protein Grams: 22

Fat Grams: 15

Total Carbohydrates Grams: 14

Net Carbohydrates Grams: 14

The Ingredients:

Tempeh – 1 pound

Maple syrup – 1 tablespoon

Soy sauce - .25 cup

Olive oil – 1 tablespoon

Liquid smoke – 1 teaspoon

The Instructions:

- Slice the tempeh into small bacon-line strips approximately one-quarter of an inch thick each.
- In a small glass, dish, whisk together the liquid smoke, soy sauce, and maple syrup until combined and then toss in the tempeh strips. Allow this mixture to marinate together for five minutes.
- Meanwhile, put a large non-stick skillet on the stove and allow it to preheat over medium.

- Into the skillet pour the olive oil so that you allow it to coat the entire bottom and then place the tempeh strips in the skillet. Cook each side of the tempeh strips until crispy and browned, about five to eight minutes for each side.

- Use the excess marinade from the container to baste the tempeh bacon during the cooking process. Don't skip this step, as it increases flavor and prevents the tempeh from drying out.

- Serve the tempeh bacon immediately or place it in the fridge to chill for up to a week before enjoying.

Lasagna Soup

This soup uses Explore Cuisine's green lentil lasagna noodles for a pack of protein and nutrients, which you can buy online. You will love how these noodles have the same texture and flavor of traditional pasta, but with a protein boost.

The Details:

The Number of Servings: 3

The Time Needed to Prepare: 5 minutes

The Time Required to Cook: 35 minutes

The Total Preparation/Cook Time: 40 minutes

Number of Calories in Individual Servings: 491

Protein Grams: 35

Fat Grams: 12

Total Carbohydrates Grams: 78

Net Carbohydrates Grams: 60

The Ingredients:

- Vegetable broth – 2 cups
- Portobello mushrooms, gills removed and finely diced – 8 ounces
- Onion powder – 1 teaspoon
- Crushed tomatoes – 28 ounces
- Diced tomatoes – 28 ounces
- Olive oil – 2 tablespoons
- Garlic, minced – 4 cloves
- Basil, fresh, chopped - .33 cup
- Nutritional yeast – 2 tablespoons
- Sea salt – 1 teaspoon
- Lentil Lasagna noodles (Explore Cuisine) – 8 ounces
- Vegan mozzarella shreds - .66 cup
- Thyme, dried – 1 teaspoon

The Instructions:

1. Into a large pot with a heavy bottom pour the olive oil and allow it to heat over medium-high. Add in the diced mushrooms and cook while stirring regularly for eight minutes. Pour the diced tomatoes, garlic,

96

and basil into the pot and continue to cook for four minutes.

2.   Into the soup pot, add the crushed tomatoes, onion powder, thyme, nutritional yeast, and vegetable broth. Bring this mixture to a boil. Break the lasagna noodles into bite-sized pieces and add them into the pot. Reduce the heat, fit on a lid, and allow the soup to simmer on low for twenty minutes.

3.   Serve the soup topped with the vegan mozzarella shreds.

Asparagus Pesto & Zucchini Noodles

The Details

Servings: 2

Nutritional Macros – One Serving:

- Calories: 311
- Fat Content: 27 grams
- Protein Count: 8 grams
- Net Carbs: 7 grams

The Ingredients:

- *The Pasta:*

- Olive oil (1 tsp.)

- Thick asparagus spears (4 ends trimmed – sliced on an angle)
- Salt and pepper (to taste)
- Zucchinis (2 medium)
- Jarred vegan pesto or homemade (.25 cup)
- *The Pesto:*
- Olive oil (3-4 tbsp.)
- Basil leaves – packed (3 cups)
- Pine nuts (1.5 tbsp.)
- Salt and pepper
- Minced garlic (1 clove)

The Instructions:

1. If you're making homemade pesto, toss all of the fixings into a food processor. Blitz it until the pesto is creamy. Set it aside for now.
2. Warm the oil in a frying pan using the med-high heat setting. Once the oil is shimmering, toss in the asparagus, salt, and pepper. Cook for five to seven minutes or until the asparagus is bright green, fork-tender, and browned.

3. Spiralize the zucchinis and mix it all together and toss well. Set aside.
4. Divide the pasta into bowls and serve or store in the fridge for another time.

Basil Risotto
Instant Pot

The Details:

Servings: 6

Nutritional Macros – One Serving:

- Calories: 260
- Fat Content: 5 grams
- Protein Count: 7.8 grams
- Net Carbs: 44 grams

The Ingredients:

- Chopped onion (1)

- Olive oil (1.5 tbsp.)
- Veggie broth (28 oz.)
- Arborio rice (12 oz.)
- Chopped basil (1.5 cups)

The Instructions:

1. Warm up the oil using the sauté mode on the Instant Pot.
2. Chop the onions and add to the cooker to sauté for three minutes. Mix in the rice and continue cooking for about one minute. Pour in the broth, stir, and secure the lid.
3. Set the timer for 15 minutes.
4. When the timer buzzes, quick-release the pressure and sauté for one minute before serving.

Eggplant Burgers – Instant Pot

The Details:

Servings: 4

Nutritional Macros – One Serving:

- Calories: 170
- Fat Content: 36 grams
- Protein Count: 15 grams
- Net Carbs: 20 grams

The Ingredients:

- Water (1 cup)
- Olive oil (2 tbsp.)
- Panko breadcrumbs (.5 cup)

- Large eggplant (1)
- Mustard (2 tbsp.)

The Instructions:

1. Add the water to the Instant Pot. Rinse and trim the eggplant and slice it into four rounds. Arrange in the cooker and secure the top. Set the timer for two minutes using the high setting.
2. When it's done, quick-release the pressure and drain the eggplant, discarding the liquid.
3. Brush them with the mustard and a coating of panko.
4. Add the oil to the pot and arrange the 'burgers' to cook using the sauté mode.
5. Cool to store in the fridge or freeze for longer shelf life.
6. Serve the burger with or without a bun.

Healthy Keto Lo Mein

The Details:

Servings: 1 large

Nutritional Macros – One Serving:

- Calories: 195
- Fat Content: 14 grams
- Protein Count: 5 grams
- Net Carbs: 4.4 grams

The Ingredients:

- Kelp noodles (1 pkg.)
- Shredded carrots (2 tbsp.)
- Frozen broccoli (1 cup)

- *For the Sauce*:
- Garlic powder (.5 tsp.)
- Tamari (2 tbsp.)
- Sesame oil (1 tbsp.)
- Ground ginger (.5 tsp.)
- Sriracha/your preference chili pepper (.25 tsp.)

The Instructions:

1. Open the noodles to soak them in water.
2. In a saucepan, using the med-low heat setting, toss in each of the sauce fixings, and the broccoli.
3. Drain the noodles. Once the pan is hot, add the noodles and cover.
4. Simmer for a few minutes, occasionally stirring the noodles. Mix in a few tablespoons of water as needed.
5. Once the noodles have softened, mix everything until ingredients are well-distributed.
6. Extinguish the heat, and leave the noodles in the pan until all the liquid in the bottom has been absorbed before serving.

Herb-Crusted Tofu

The Details:

Servings: 6 – 2 steaks

Nutritional Macros – One Serving:

- Calories: 150
- Fat Content: 8 grams
- Protein Count: 12 grams
- Net Carbs: 5 grams

The Ingredients:

- Extra-firm tofu (28 oz./2 blocks)
- Olive oil (2 tbsp.)
- Quinoa flour (.25 cup)
- Nutritional yeast (.5 cup)

- Smoked paprika (.25 tsp.)
- Sage (1 tsp.)
- Italian seasoning (1 tbsp.)
- Dried garlic (1 tsp.)
- Salt and black pepper (as desired)

The Instructions:

1. Warm the oven at 400° Fahrenheit.
2. Cut the tofu into steaks, about ½-inch thick. Each block should get you about six steaks. Set them aside.
3. In a shallow dish, whisk the dry fixings.
4. Now, prepare an assembly line. Put the olive oil in another shallow dish.
5. First, cover a tofu steak in oil. Then place the tofu in the bowl of the dry fixings and coat the tofu with the dry mixture.
6. Arrange the steak on a baking tin and repeat with the remainder of the tofu.
7. When it's ready to bake, set a timer for 15 minutes, then flip and continue cooking it until it's golden brown and crispy (15-20 min.).
8. Serve the tofu with your favorite sauce and your favorite vegetable side dish.

Lentil Quinoa Meatloaf

The Details:

Servings: 8

Nutritional Macros – One Serving:

- Calories: 189
- Fat Content: 6 grams
- Protein Count: 9 grams
- Net Carbs: 13 grams

The Ingredients:

- Diced carrots (1 cup)
- Chopped mushrooms (1 cup)
- Diced shallots (.25 cup)

- Garlic cloves (2 minced)
- Cooked lentils – separated (1.5 cups) – (from about .5 cup dry)
- Walnuts (.5 cup)
- Cooked quinoa – ex. Red Mill (.75 cup)
- Oats (1.5 cups)
- Tomato paste (3 tbsp.)
- Hot sauce (1 tsp.)
- Gluten-free tamari (2 tbsp.)
- Flaxseed meal (1 tbsp.)
- Nutritional yeast (3 tbsp.)
- Maple syrup (1 tbsp.)
- Miso paste (1 tsp.)
- Italian seasoning – basil -oregano – thyme – parsley (total of 2 tsp.)
- Salt and pepper (as desired)
- *The Glaze:*
- Tomato paste (2 tbsp.)
- Apple cider vinegar (2 tsp.)
- Gluten-free tamari (.5 tsp.)
- Maple syrup (2 tsp.)
- Ground mustard (.5 tsp.)
- Also Needed: 9 by 5-inch loaf pan

The Instructions:

1. Warm the oven to reach 350ºFahrenheit. Cover the pan with parchment baking paper and set it aside.

2. Sauté the carrots, mushrooms, shallots, salt, pepper, and garlic in a large skillet, until the carrots are tender, about five minutes.

3. Dump the mixture into a food processor and add the remainder of the fixings, reserving ½ cup of lentils. Process it to create the dough. Pulse in the rest of the lentils.

4. Place the loaf into the pan, pressing it down with a wooden spoon.

5. Whisk the glaze fixings and pour it over the loaf. Cover the pan with foil and bake for 20 minutes. Discard the foil and bake uncovered for an additional five minutes.

6. Cool the meatloaf for five minutes before slicing.

7. The remaining slices can be kept in the fridge for two to three days or frozen. Why not make a double batch and freeze it for another time?

Mexican Black Bean Enchiladas With Butternut Squash

The Details

Servings: 8

Nutritional Macros – One Serving:

- Calories: 222
- Fat Content: 8 grams
- Protein Count: 7 grams
- Net Carbs: 22 grams

The Ingredients:

- Cubed butternut squash (2 cups)
- Black beans (15 oz. can)
- Jarred salsa – your preference (.25 cup)

- Corn tortillas (8)
- Enchilada sauce (1-1.5 cups)

The Sauce:

- Olive oil (2 tbsp.)
- Garlic (.5 tsp.)
- Smoked paprika (.5 tsp.)
- Chili powder (1.5 tbsp.)
- Cumin (2 tsp.)
- Onion powder (.5 tsp.)
- Salt (1 pinch)
- Quinoa/grain-based flour – your preference (2 tbsp.)
- Tomato paste (.25 cup)
- Veggie broth (2 cups)

The Instructions:

1. Set the oven temperature to reach 375º Fahrenheit. Rinse and drain the beans.
2. Warm the oil in a small pan using the med-low setting. At that time, whisk in the flour, spices, and tomato paste until thickened.
3. Gently pour in half the veggie broth, whisking until it's creamy. Simmer for two to three minutes. Pour in the rest of the broth and simmer

for an additional two to three minutes until it's slightly thickened. Turn off the burner and set the pan to the side for now.

4. Prepare the filling. Cube the squash and toss it into a large pan and with a splash or two of water. Cover the pan and steam the squash for five to seven minutes. Once tender, dump in the salsa and beans to cook until warmed thoroughly.

5. Add ¼ cup of sauce to a baking dish. Add two to three tablespoons of filling to the tortilla and roll it up, arranging them seam-side down in the baking container.

6. Pour the rest of the sauce across the tortillas with a dusting of the cheese.

7. Arrange the dish onto the center oven rack and bake until the cheese is melted (25 to 30 min.).

8. Remove them from the oven and wait for five minutes.

9. Serve and garnish with your favorite toppings.

10. For meal prep, cool the dish and store in the fridge or portion it into a meal prep container for later.

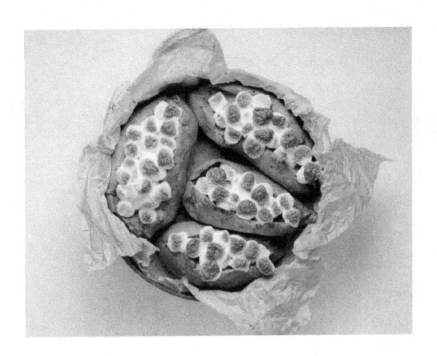

Stuffed Potatoes With Salsa & Beans

The Details:

Servings: 4

Nutritional Macros – One Serving:

- Calories: 324
- Fat Content: 8 grams
- Protein Count: 9.2 grams
- Net Carbs: 40.7 grams

The Ingredients:

- Medium russet potatoes (4)
- Fresh salsa (.5 cup)
- Ripe avocado (1)
- Pinto beans (15 oz. can)
- Chopped pickled jalapeños (4 tsp.)

The Instructions:

1. Poke the potatoes using a skewer or fork.
2. *Prep the Potatoes*: Option 1: Set the oven at 425º Fahrenheit and bake the potatoes at until tender (45 min.-1 hr.) . Option 2: Microwave for 20 minutes using medium power, turning once or twice, until softened (20 min.). Transfer them to a chopping block to cool slightly.
3. Make a lengthwise cut to open the potato, but don't cut all the way through. Pinch the ends to expose the flesh.
4. Rinse, warm, and lightly mash the beans. Slice the avocado.
5. Top each potato with some salsa, avocado, beans, and jalapeños. Serve warm.

Zucchini Meatballs

The Details:

Servings: 12 meatballs

Nutritional Macros – One Serving:

- Calories: 71
- Fat Content: 6.6 grams
- Protein Count: 1.7 grams
- Net Carbs: 1.1 grams

The Ingredients:

- Shredded zucchini (1 cup)
- Chopped or ground walnuts – depending on your preference (1 cup)
- Salt (.25 tsp.)

- Italian seasoning (1 tbsp.)
- Psyllium husks (1 tbsp.)
- Granulated garlic (.25 tsp.)
- Red pepper flakes (.25 tsp.)
- Dried oregano (1 tbsp.)

The Instructions:

1. Heat the oven at 350° Fahrenheit. Prepare a baking tray using a layer of parchment baking paper.
2. Stir together the grated zucchini, chopped walnuts, and salt. Wait for about five minutes for some of the moisture to be pulled out of the zucchini.
3. Add in the seasoning and psyllium, and mix until thoroughly combined. Wait for another five minutes, so the psyllium can start to bind.
4. Form golf ball-sized balls and arrange them on the baking tray.
5. Set a timer and bake the meatballs until they are firm to the touch and browned or for 30 to 35 minutes.

6. Combine the meatballs with a portion of zucchini or shirataki noodles using a low carb red sauce, and serve.

Peanut Butter Overnight Oats

These overnight oats are a great option for a quick meal on-the-go. You simply prepare these oats the night before you plan to enjoy them, or up to a week before, and then you can easily pull them out of the fridge whenever you need a quick meal.

The Details:

The Number of Servings: 2

The Time Needed to Prepare: 5 minutes

The Time Required to Cook: 0 minutes

The Total Preparation/Cook Time: 5 minutes

Number of Calories in Individual Servings: 507

Protein Grams: 17

Fat Grams: 16

Total Carbohydrates Grams: 76

Net Carbohydrates Grams: 62

The Ingredients:

- Maple syrup – 2 tablespoons
- Rolled oats - .75 cup
- Dairy-free milk, unsweetened (soy, almond, or coconut) – 1 cup
- Vanilla extract – 1 teaspoon
- Water - .5 cup
- Chia seeds – 2 tablespoons
- Banana, mashed – 1
- Cinnamon - .5 teaspoon
- Peanut butter – 2 tablespoons

The Instructions:

1. In a kitchen bowl that is of medium size, incorporate together the chia seeds, rolled oats, sea salt, and cinnamon. Add in the mashed banana,

peanut butter, vanilla extract, water, and dairy-free milk.

2. Transfer the oat mixture to two pint-sized mason jars, with half of the mixture being in each jar to measure out the two individual servings.

3. Refrigerate the oats for at least four hours, or until you wake up before enjoying. Serve cold.

Corn Fritters

These corn fritters offer a decadent, yet simple, snack! In fact, they are so nice that you can serve them as a side along with a main dish for a complete meal. Enjoy these alone or dripped in a cashew "cheese" sauce.

The Details:

The Number of Servings: 4

The Time Needed to Prepare: 10 minutes

The Time Required to Cook: 17 minutes

The Total Preparation/Cook Time: 27 minutes

Number of Calories in Individual Servings: 191

Protein Grams: 3

Fat Grams: 7

Total Carbohydrates Grams: 27

Net Carbohydrates Grams: 25

The Ingredients:

- Garlic powder – 1 teaspoon
- Flour, all-purpose - .5 cup
- Cornmeal - .25 cup
- Baking powder - .5 teaspoon
- Black pepper, ground - .25 teaspoon
- Dairy-free milk, unsweetened (soy, almond, or coconut) – .5 cup, + 1 tablespoon
- Red bell pepper, diced - .5 cup
- Corn kernels – 1 cup
- Green onions, thinly sliced – 2
- Sea salt - .75 teaspoon
- Light olive oil for frying

The Instructions:

1. Line a large dinner plate or a tray with paper towels and then set it aside.
2. In a large kitchen bowl made of metal, incorporate your cornmeal, flour, black pepper, baking

powder, garlic powder, and sea salt with a whisk until all the seasonings are evenly distributed.

3.   Pour the dairy-free milk of choice into the mixture of dry ingredients and whisk just until combined, being careful to not over mix the batter. Your batter should be thick but not dry. If it turns out dry, add a tablespoon of extra milk.

4.   Fold the green onions, bell pepper, and corn kernels into the batter using a silicone spatula.

5.   Place a large non-stick skillet on a stove at medium heat until hot, about one to two minutes. Once preheated, drizzle in enough olive oil to lightly cover the entire bottom of the skillet.

6.   Use a large cookie scoop to measure out the fritter batter, or a one-quarter cup filled up approximately one-half to three-quarters of the way. Use this scoop and create small fritters in the oil, however many can fit in your skillet without touching each other. When you pour the batter in, it should be hot enough to sizzle. Gently press down on the fritter batter pound with your scoop to flatten it a bit.

7.   Cook the fritters for two to four minutes on each side until golden brown. You can use a spatula to

lightly lift the edges of the fritters to check the color on the bottom before flipping.

8.   Once both sides of the fritters have finished cooking, place them on the kitchen dinner plate that has been lined with paper towels to remove excess oil and continue to fry up the remaining batter. Add more oil to the skillet as needed.

Peanut Butter Energy Bites

These energy bites are the perfect replacement for dairy-filled energy bars, and just as delicious! Feel free to make minor changes to alter the flavor, such as adding in chocolate chips, coconut flakes, or raisins.

The Details:

The Number of Servings: 6

The Time Needed to Prepare: 10 minutes

The Time Required to Cook: 0 minutes

The Total Preparation/Cook Time: 10 minutes

Number of Calories in Individual Servings: 271

Protein Grams: 9

Fat Grams: 16

Total Carbohydrates Grams: 24

Net Carbohydrates Grams: 22

The Ingredients:

- Oat flour - .5 cup
- Peanut butter, smooth - .75 cup
- Maple syrup – 5 tablespoons
- Vanilla extract – 2 teaspoons

The Instructions:

1.   In a medium-sized kitchen, bowl, whisk together to incorporate well the smooth peanut butter along with the pure maple syrup and genuine vanilla extract. Add in the oat flour and continue to stir until it is thick and evenly distributed.

2.   Prepare a large aluminum baking sheet by lining it with parchment paper or a silicone kitchen mat.

3.   Use a tablespoon to scoop out evenly sized bites and roll each tablespoon portion between your hands to form a sphere. As you prepare the bites to place them on the prepared baking sheet so that their

edges do not touch. Place this pan in the freezer and allow them to chill for thirty minutes until set.

4.   Once removed from the freezer, the bites will be firmer so you can roll them between your palms again if their shape is not round enough.

5.   Place the bites in a plastic bag or another plastic or glass container and set them in either the fridge or freezer.

Cookie Dough Dip

It may sound weird to make cookie dough dip with white beans, but you would be surprised how amazing this taste! White beans on their own have a very subtle flavor, so when you add in the other ingredients, you can't taste them at all. Yet, the beans add both nutrition and protein, making this a delicious and guilt-free sweet treat.

The Details:

The Number of Servings: 6

The Time Needed to Prepare: 5 minutes

The Time Required to Cook: 0 minutes

The Total Preparation/Cook Time: 5 minutes

Number of Calories in Individual Servings: 252

Protein Grams: 7

Fat Grams: 10

Total Carbohydrates Grams: 34

Net Carbohydrates Grams: 26

The Ingredients:

- White beans, rinsed well – 1 can
- Cashew butter – 2 tablespoons
- Ground flaxseeds – 2 tablespoons
- Dairy-free milk, unsweetened (soy, almond, or coconut) – 2 tablespoons
- Maple syrup – .25 cup
- Chocolate chips, dairy-free - .5 cup
- Vanilla extract – 1 teaspoon

The Instructions:

- Except for the chocolate chips, place all the ingredients in a food processor and allow it to blend until it creates a smooth batter. Use a spoon and stir in the chocolate chips.

- Pour the batter into a bowl and serve as a dip along with fruit, cookies, or vegan graham crackers.

Oatmeal Raisin Energy Bites

These energy bites have a flavor like oatmeal raisin cookies, making them delicious! Although, if you don't care for raisins, you could always replace them with chocolate chips instead. Just be sure that the chocolate you use is dairy-free.

The Details:

The Number of Servings: 6

The Time Needed to Prepare: 10 minutes

The Time Required to Cook: 0 minutes

The Total Preparation/Cook Time: 10 minutes

Number of Calories in Individual Servings: 226

Protein Grams: 4

Fat Grams: 7

Total Carbohydrates Grams: 45

Net Carbohydrates Grams: 39

The Ingredients:

- Rolled oats - .75 cup
- Raisins - .5 cup
- Walnuts - .5 cup
- Medjool dates pitted – 12

The Instructions:

1. Place your walnuts and raisins into a food processor and blend until both ingredients have been roughly chopped. Add in the Medjool dates and continue to pulse the mixture until the dates have become finely chopped and mushy.

2. Add the rolled oats to the food processor and continue to pulse until they are evenly incorporated.

3. The mixture should stick together easily when you squeeze it together without sticking to your hands too much. If the mixture is not sticky enough, add a few more dates. If it is too sticky, add a little more oatmeal.

4. Use a tablespoon to measure out your bites and form each tablespoon's serving between your palms to create a sphere. Once done, place the bites in a container and store in the fridge until use.

Chocolate Almond Granola

This granola is great for a snack on-the-go or a quick breakfast when you are tight on time. Granola is incredibly versatile, so if you want to experiment, you could try adding in some of your favorite dried fruits or coconut.

The Details:

The Number of Servings: 5

The Time Needed to Prepare: 10 minutes

The Time Required to Cook: 20 minutes

The Total Preparation/Cook Time: 30 minutes

Number of Calories in Individual Servings: 380

Protein Grams: 12

Fat Grams: 19

Total Carbohydrates Grams: 43

Net Carbohydrates Grams: 36

The Ingredients:

- Rolled oats – 1.25 cups
- Almond butter - .33 cup
- Sea salt - .25 teaspoon
- Vanilla extract – .5 teaspoon
- Cocoa powder – .5 tablespoon
- Maple syrup – 3 tablespoons
- Almonds, roasted - .25 cup
- Chocolate chips, dairy-free - .25 cup

The Instructions:

1. Preheat your oven to a temperature of Fahrenheit three-hundred and twenty-five degrees and then line a large aluminum baking sheet with kitchen parchment or a cooking silicone mat.

2. In a large bowl, whisk to incorporate together the smooth almond butter and pure maple syrup. However, if your almond butter is too difficult to stir, you can first microwave it. Add in the vanilla extract,

sea salt, and cocoa powder and stir with a spoon until it is fully combined.

3.   Pour the oats and almonds into the prepared mixture and toss them together until they are all combined and well coated. Spread this mixture over the prepared baking sheet.

4.   Place the chocolate almond granola on the baking sheet in the preheated oven and allow it to bake for twenty minutes, stirring the mixture once halfway through the cooking process.

5.   Once the granola has cooled to room temperature, stir in the chocolate chips and store in an airtight container.

Lemon Loaf Cake

This lemon loaf cake is simple and quick to make, but fresh and full of zesty flavor! Enjoy the cake on its own or use it in place of pound cake when making parfaits and other desserts.

The Details:

The Number of Servings: 8

The Time Needed to Prepare: 15 minutes

The Time Required to Cook: 1 hour

The Total Preparation/Cook Time: 75 minutes

Number of Calories in Individual Servings: 364

Protein Grams: 3

Fat Grams: 13

Total Carbohydrates Grams: 56

Net Carbohydrates Grams: 56

The Ingredients:

- Flour, all-purpose – 2 cups
- Lemon zest – 2 tablespoons
- Sea salt - .5 teaspoon
- Sugar, granulated - .75 cup
- Dairy-free milk, unsweetened (soy, almond, or coconut) – 1 cup
- Light olive oil - .5 cup
- Lemon juice - .25 cup
- Vanilla extract – 1 teaspoon
- Baking powder – 1 tablespoon
- Powdered sugar – 1 cup
- Lemon juice – 2 tablespoons
- Lemon zest – 1 teaspoon
- Sea salt - .25 teaspoon

The Instructions:

1.   Begin by preheating your oven to a temperature of Fahrenheit three-hundred and fifty degrees and

ensuring the metal rack is placed in the center of the oven. Prepare a nine-inch by five-inch loaf pan by greasing and flouring it or lining it with kitchen parchment before setting it aside.

2.   In a medium-sized kitchen, bowl combine with a whisk or spoon the all-purpose flour, half teaspoon of sea salt, and baking powder.

3.   In a large bowl, whisk together the sugar, dairy-free milk, light olive oil, one-quarter cup of lemon juice, vanilla extract, and two tablespoons of lemon zest.

4.   Slowly whisk the flour mixture into the liquid mixture until it is fully incorporated. Don't over mix the matter.

5.   Pour the vegan lemon loaf cake batter into the loaf pan you had previously prepared and then placed it in the middle of your oven to bake for forty minutes. After this time is up, temporarily remove the loaf pan from the oven and cover the top of the cake with aluminum foil to prevent the top from burning.

6.   Placed the loaf pan with aluminum foil back in the oven for fifteen to twenty minutes until you can insert a toothpick into the center of the loaf, and it comes out clean.

7. Once removed from the oven, set the loaf pan on a wire cooling rack, and allow it to cool at room temperature. Once cool enough to handle, remove the cake from the parchment and allow it to finish cooling completely on the wire rack.

8. After the cake reaches room temperature, whisk together the powder sugar and remaining lemon juice, zest, and sea salt until no clumps remain. Drizzle the glaze over the cake loaf and allow it to set for ten to twenty minutes. You can chill it in the fridge to get the glaze to set more quickly.

9. Slice the cake into eight portions and enjoy!

Carrot Bundt Cake

This cake is simple to make, yet full of flavor and can easily feed a crowd. Whether you are enjoying this cake for a birthday, at the holidays, or for a potluck, everyone will be pleased to enjoy this flavorful sweet carrot cake. While golden raisins are used in this recipe for their mild flavor and appearance, feel free to use regular raisins, if you desire.

The Details:

The Number of Servings: 15

The Time Needed to Prepare: 15 minutes

The Time Required to Cook: 60 minutes

The Total Preparation/Cook Time: 75 minutes

Number of Calories in Individual Servings: 331

Protein Grams: 4

Fat Grams: 14

Total Carbohydrates Grams: 46

Net Carbohydrates Grams: 44

The Ingredients:

- Dairy-free milk, unsweetened (soy, almond, or coconut) – .33 cup
- Cinnamon – 2 teaspoons
- White vinegar – 1 teaspoon
- Egg replacement, prepared (Bob's Red Mill or Ener-G) – 3
- Light olive oil - .5 cup
- Raisins, golden - .5 cup
- Apple sauce, unsweetened - .5 cup
- Vanilla extract – 1 teaspoon
- Sugar, granulated – 1.5 cup
- Flour, all-purpose – 2 cups
- Sea salt - .5 teaspoon
- Baking soda – 1 teaspoon
- Carrots, shredded – 2 cups
- Walnuts, chopped – 1 cup

- Powdered sugar - .75 cup
- Vanilla extract – 1 teaspoon
- Vegan cream cheese - .25 cup
- Margarine (Earth Balance) – 3 tablespoons
- Baking powder – 2 teaspoons

The Instructions:

1. Begin by preheating your oven to a temperature of Fahrenheit three-hundred and fifty degrees and ensuring the metal rack is placed in the center of the oven. Fully grease the inside of a bundt pan, including the center rod, to prevent sticking. Set the pan aside while you prepare your batter.

2. In a medium-sized kitchen bowl, combine together with a small spoon the dairy-free milk and vinegar. Allow this mixture to sit for two to five minutes to allow it to become buttermilk.

3. Once the buttermilk has sat add in the prepared vegan egg, olive oil, applesauce, cinnamon, sea salt, and one teaspoon of vanilla extract. Once combined, add in the sugar, all-purpose flour, baking powder, and baking soda. Mix it just until combined, being careful to not over mix.

4.   Gently fold the carrots, raisins, and walnuts into the cake batter.

5.   Pour the prepared batter into the bundt pan and place it in the oven, allowing it to cook until a toothpick pressed in the center of the carrot bundt cake is removed clean of batter, about fifty to sixty minutes.

6.   After removing the bundt pan from the oven, place it on a wire cooling rack for fifteen minutes to cool at room temperature. Once it is cool enough to handle gently, remove the cake from the pan and allow it to fully cool.

7.   Once the cake has cooled to room temperature, beat together the powdered sugar, vegan cream cheese, margarine, and one teaspoon of vanilla with an electric beater. Once creamy and without clumps, ice the cooled cake and serve.

Chewy Chocolate Brownies

Who doesn't love a good brownie? You can enjoy these brownies on their own or take them to the next level by serving them with vegan ice cream, coconut whipped cream, or even caramel sauce. The options are endless!

The Details:

The Number of Servings: 8

The Time Needed to Prepare: 10 minutes

The Time Required to Cook: 25 minutes

The Total Preparation/Cook Time: 35 minutes

Number of Calories in Individual Servings: 396

Protein Grams: 6

Fat Grams: 16

Total Carbohydrates Grams: 61

Net Carbohydrates Grams: 56

The Ingredients:

- Flaxseed, ground – 1 tablespoon
- Water, warm – 2.5 tablespoons
- Flour, all-purpose - .75 cup
- Almond flour – 1 cup
- Cocoa powder – 8 tablespoons
- Baking soda - .25 teaspoon
- Sea salt - .5 teaspoon
- Sugar, granulated – 1.5 cups
- Water - .25 cup
- Vanilla extract – 1 teaspoon
- Margarine (Earth Balance) - .25 cup
- Chocolate chips, dairy-free - .75 cup

The Instructions:

1.   Begin by preheating your oven to a temperature of Fahrenheit three-hundred and fifty degrees and ensuring the metal rack is placed in the center of the oven. Grease and line an eight-inch square baking dish with kitchen parchment and then set it aside.

2. Prepare a flax egg by whisking together the ground flaxseed and two and a half tablespoons of warm water until no clumps remain. Allow the mixture to sit for about two minutes to thicken to an egg-like consistency.

3. In a medium-sized kitchen bowl, whisk together the all-purpose flour, almond flour, baking soda, and sea salt. Set aside.

4. In a small microwave-safe glass dish, melt the margarine with two-thirds of the chocolate chips (half a cup), cocoa powder, and one-quarter cup of water. Melt this mixture in increments of thirty seconds, stirring it well after each increment until fully melted and combined.

5. Add the vanilla extract and sugar to the melted chocolate mixture until combined. Stir in the prepared flaxseed egg.

6. Pour the melted chocolate mixture into the prepared flour mixture and stir just until combined, being careful to not over mix the batter. The batter will be thick.

7. Fold in the remaining one-quarter cup of chocolate chips and then pour the batter into the prepared square baking dish. Place the pan in the

oven and allow it to cook until set but still gooey, about twenty-five to thirty minutes.

8.   Remove the vegan chewy chocolate brownies from the center of the oven and allow them to cool at room temperature for twenty to thirty minutes before slicing.

Classic Peanut Butter Cookies

Sometimes simplicity is the best. While you can certainly enjoy cakes, donuts, and other treats from this chapter, sometimes you want a dessert that only takes a few minutes to bake. These cookies are delicious and full of the rich peanut flavor we all crave of this classic treat. Enjoy these cookies alone or dipped in dairy-free chocolate.

The Details:

The Number of Servings: 12

The Time Needed to Prepare: 8 minutes

The Time Required to Cook: 12 minutes

The Total Preparation/Cook Time: 20 minutes

Number of Calories in Individual Servings: 264

Protein Grams: 6

Fat Grams: 14

Total Carbohydrates Grams: 30

Net Carbohydrates Grams: 29

The Ingredients:

- Baking powder - .5 teaspoon
- Peanut butter, creamy, unsweetened – 1 cup
- Vanilla extract – 1 teaspoon
- Margarine, room temperature (Earth Balance) - .5 cup
- Brown sugar - .5 cup
- Sugar, granulated - .5 cup
- Dairy-free milk, unsweetened (soy, almond, or coconut) – .25 cup
- Flour, all-purpose - 1 cups
- Sea salt - .25 teaspoon
- Baking soda – 1 teaspoon

The Instructions:

- Begin by preheating your oven to a temperature of Fahrenheit three-hundred and fifty degrees and ensuring the metal rack is placed in the center of the oven. Line a large aluminum kitchen baking sheet with kitchen parchment or a silicone baking mat to prevent sticking.

- In a medium-sized kitchen bowl, use a whisk to completely combine together the all-purpose flour, sea salt, baking soda, and baking powder until it's evenly combined. Set the bowl aside.

- In another kitchen bowl, use an electric hand beater to whip together the margarine and smooth and creamy unsweetened peanut butter until it is fully combined and creamy. Beat in both the sugar and brown sugar before beating again. Lastly, beat in the dairy-free milk and vanilla extract.

- Add the flour mixture into the peanut butter mixture and combine them both together until both mixtures are evenly and fully incorporated. Be careful to not over mix.

- Using a cookie dough scoop (which holds two tablespoons of dough) or a large spoon scoop out evenly sized cookie dough balls and place them on the parchment paper two inches apart each. Don't place them too close together, or they will expand and stick together while cooking.

- Use a fork to gently press into the top of the cookies, making two indentations into the top in a crisscross pattern. This will slightly flatten the cookies but be careful to not press them down too much, as you want them to remain thick.

- Place the baking sheet in the preheated oven and allow the cookies to bake until the edges begin to firm, but the center is still soft, about twelve to fifteen minutes.

- Allow the classic peanut butter cookies to cool on the pan they were baked on for five minutes before removing them and allowing them to finish cooling on a wire cooling rack.

Thumbprint Cookies

This classic teatime treat is not only simple to make, but they are fun to create, as well! Children will especially enjoy helping to prepare these cookies. With a shortbread cookie base, the flavor options are incredibly versatile, allowing you to use any of your favorite jams! A few classic jam options are raspberry, strawberry, and lemon curd. But, if you use lemon curd, be sure that it is a vegan variety.

The Details:

The Number of Servings: 12

The Time Needed to Prepare: 15 minutes

The Time Required to Cook: 15 minutes

The Total Preparation/Cook Time: 30 minutes

Number of Calories in Individual Servings: 219

Protein Grams: 2

Fat Grams: 9

Total Carbohydrates Grams: 30

Net Carbohydrates Grams: 30

The Ingredients:

- Flour, all-purpose – 2 cups
- Sea salt - .5 teaspoon
- Sugar, granulated - .5 cup
- Dairy-free milk, unsweetened (soy, almond, or coconut) – 2 tablespoons
- Margarine, softened (Earth Balance) - .75 cup
- Almond extract - .5 teaspoon
- Vanilla extract – 1 teaspoon
- Jam of choice - .33 cup

The Instructions:

1. Begin by preheating your oven to a temperature of Fahrenheit three-hundred and fifty degrees and ensuring the metal rack is placed in the center of the oven. Line a large baking sheet with kitchen parchment or a silicone baking mat to prevent sticking.

2. In a medium-sized kitchen bowl, whisk together the sea salt and flour and then set it aside.

3. In another bowl, beat the margarine with an electric beater until it is light and creamy. Add in the sugar and once again whip until incorporated before adding in the almond and vanilla extracts.

4. With the electric beater on low speed, slowly add in the flour mixture and beat it just until incorporated, being sure to not overbeat the mixture. Add in the dairy-free milk and mix just until combined.

5. Use a half tablespoon to scoop out small portions of dough, and then roll each of these portions into a small dough ball. Place each dough ball on the prepared baking sheet one and a half inches apart.

6. With your finger or the back of a one-quarter teaspoon press an indentation into the center of each dough ball. Don't press all the way down, or the cookie will develop a hole for the jam to leak through. Instead, press the indentation halfway through the dough ball.

7. Using a small spoon, add a small amount of jam to the center of each cookie, being careful to not overfill or it will overflow and burn during the baking process.

8.   Bake the cookies until the edges just begin to set, and the bottoms begin to turn golden. Don't over bake them, or they will turn out crispy. They should bake twelve to fifteen minutes.

9.   After removing the cookies from the oven, allow them to cool on the baking sheet for five minutes before carefully transferring them to a wire cooling rack to finish cooling.

Peach Crisp

This crisp is delicious and perfect with peaches that are in-season. However, you can also enjoy this made with ripe pears, apples, berries, or even plums. Crisp is incredibly versatile and can be enjoyed with any fruit that bakes well.

The Details:

The Number of Servings: 6

The Time Needed to Prepare: 7 minutes

The Time Required to Cook: 30 minutes

The Total Preparation/Cook Time: 37 minutes

Number of Calories in Individual Servings: 339

Protein Grams: 4

Fat Grams: 18

Total Carbohydrates Grams: 41

Net Carbohydrates Grams: 38

The Ingredients:

- Peaches, ripe – 5
- Cornstarch – 1 tablespoon
- Nutmeg, ground - .125 teaspoon
- Vanilla extract - .5 teaspoon
- Lemon juice – 1.5 teaspoon
- Sugar, granulated – 1.5 tablespoons
- Rolled oats - .5 cup
- Flour, all-purpose - .5 cup
- Margarine (Earth Balance) .66 cup
- Sugar, granulated - .25 cup
- Cinnamon – .25 teaspoon
- Sea salt - .125 teaspoon
- Vanilla extract - .5 teaspoon

The Instructions:

1.	Begin by preheating your oven to a temperature of Fahrenheit three-hundred and fifty degrees and ensuring the metal rack is placed in the center of the oven. Grease and line an eight-inch square baking dish with kitchen parchment and then set it aside.

2.   Peel and slice the peaches, with the slices being approximately one-quarter to one-half of an inch in thickness each. Place the sliced peaches into a kitchen bowl along with the Cornstarch, one and a half tablespoons of sugar, lemon juice, nutmeg, and half teaspoon of vanilla. Toss the ingredients together until the peaches are fully coated and then set aside.

3.   In another bowl, use a fork to combine the rolled oats, flour, remaining sugar, sea salt, and cinnamon. Once combined, use the fork or a pastry cutter to mix in the margarine to form a crumble topping.

4.   Spread the peach mixture into the prepared baking dish and then evenly crumble the oat topping over the peaches. Slightly pat the crumble down so that it sticks to the peaches before placing the dish in the oven.

5.   Allow the crisp to bake in the oven until the crumble is golden and the peaches are soft, about twenty-five to thirty minutes. Serve while warm.

Rice Pudding

Rice pudding is a comforting and creamy dessert that can be enjoyed either hot or cold. Enjoy plain or try adding in some cardamom or serving with a topping of caramel sauce.

The Details:

The Number of Servings: 4

The Time Needed to Prepare: 10 minutes

The Time Required to Cook: 50 minutes

The Total Preparation/Cook Time: 60 minutes

Number of Calories in Individual Servings: 281

Protein Grams: 5

Fat Grams: 1

Total Carbohydrates Grams: 60

Net Carbohydrates Grams: 59

The Ingredients:

- Basmati white rice - .75 cup
- Soymilk – 1.66 cup
- Water – 1 cup
- Sugar, granulated - .25 cup
- Brown sugar - .25 cup
- Vanilla extract - .5 teaspoon
- Sea salt - .5 teaspoon
- Cinnamon, ground - .5 teaspoon
- Margarine (Earth Bound) – 2 tablespoons

The Instructions:

1. In a large pot with a heavy bottom combine the Basmati rice, soy milk, both sugars, water, and sea salt. Turn the heat of the large pot to a medium-high on the stove and bring it to a bubbling boil while stirring frequently.

2. Once the soy milk and water mixture reaches a bubbling boil, turn the heat down to a temperature of low, cover the pot with a lid, and allow it to lightly simmer. Stir the mixture frequently to prevent

sticking and burning until the rice is tender and it develops a thick custard consistency, about fifty minutes.

3.   Remove the rice pudding from the heat and stir in the margarine, vanilla extract, and cinnamon. Serve while hot or cold.

Pumpkin Pie

The holidays are never complete without a pumpkin pie to celebrate. This classic has never been more delicious or guilt-free than before! You can enjoy your pie while knowing you are also maintaining a vegan lifestyle.

The Details:

The Number of Servings: 8

The Time Needed to Prepare: 7 minutes

The Time Required to Cook: 60 minutes

The Total Preparation/Cook Time: 67 minutes

Number of Calories in Individual Servings: 305

Protein Grams: 2

Fat Grams: 13

Total Carbohydrates Grams: 46

Net Carbohydrates Grams: 43

The Ingredients:

- Cinnamon, ground – 1 teaspoon
- Pie crust, vegan – 1
- Pumpkin puree – 15 ounces
- Ginger, ground – 1 teaspoon
- Coconut milk, full fat – 1 cup
- Cornstarch – 3 tablespoons
- Brown sugar – 1 cup
- Sea salt – .5 teaspoon
- Nutmeg, ground - .5 teaspoon
- Cloves, ground - .125 teaspoon

The Instructions:

1.   Begin by preheating your oven to a temperature of Fahrenheit three-hundred and fifty degrees and ensuring the metal rack is placed in the center of the oven.

2.   Prepare a standard nine-inch pie plate by lining it with a vegan pie crust.

3.   In a large bowl, using an electric beater to fully combine the pumpkin puree, brown sugar, coconut

milk, Cornstarch, salt, and spices until creamy and smooth. Pour this mixture into the prepared pie crust and spread it out evenly with a spatula.

4.   Place the prepared pie in the oven and allow it to bake for one hour until it has begun to set. It will still jiggle when shaken, but it will continue to set up as it cools. Allow the pie to cool at room temperature for half an hour before placing it in the fridge to chill completely before serving.

Caramel Sauce

This caramel sauce is a wonderful addition to make desserts and beverages. Whether you are topping off chewy brownies, rice pudding, peach crisp, or a cafe mocha, you are sure to love this caramel sauce!

The Details:

The Number of Servings: 8

The Time Needed to Prepare: 3 minutes

The Time Required to Cook: 7 minutes

The Total Preparation/Cook Time: 10 minutes

Number of Calories in Individual Servings: 151

Protein Grams: 0

Fat Grams: 7

Total Carbohydrates Grams: 22

Net Carbohydrates Grams: 22

The Ingredients:

- Brown sugar - .75 cup
- Coconut milk, full-fat (Thai Kitchen) – 1 cup
- Sea salt - .5 teaspoon
- Cornstarch – 1 tablespoon

The Instructions:

1. Combine all the ingredients together on a medium-sized saucepan on the stove and allow the cream of the coconut milk to melt over medium-high heat while stirring constantly.

2. Once the mixture begins to bubble and boil, lower the stove's temperature to low heat and allow the sauce to simmer for five minutes.

3. Remove the caramel from the heat and use immediately or store in the fridge and use it at your convenience.